THE GUIDE
PREPARATION FOR MARRIAGE FOR SIKH GIRLS

GURMIT KAUR

MASSIS GUIDE TO SIKH MARRIAGES
Copyright © 2015 by Gurmit Kaur.

All rights reserved. No part of this publication may be reproduced, distributed or transmitted in any form or by any means, including photocopying, recording, or other electronic or mechanical methods, without the prior written permission of the publisher, except in the case of brief quotations embodied in critical reviews and certain other noncommercial uses permitted by copyright law. For permission requests, write to the publisher, addressed "Attention: Permissions Coordinator," at the address below.

Front Cover Design: The Bride sits in the center and outside four clogs, each one represents the Wedding Lavan. The stage we have to go through before we are united with the universe and become the brides of the universe.

Copyright Paintings and Photographs by Gurmit Kaur

ISBN: 978-1-326-28631-6

FOREWORD

The world has undergone a massive transformation in the last 50 years. New technologies have replaced the entire way that marriages used to be conducted. For those who are old enough to remember, the past days are vintage.

To the newer generation, our stories may sound strange and antiquated when compared to more contemporary practices. The technological age that we have increasingly inhabited over the last 30 years or so has bought greater advances in terms of searching for a suitable match. But there is one thing that has not changed: the principle duties of those entering into marriage partnerships.

Marriage is a sacred rite of passage for two families, but it is also a harbinger of trials and tribulations. There are increasing cases of separation and divorce, lack of proper research into its causes and effects blurs clarity around these issues. Each year the global Sikh population spends billions of dollars in activities pertaining to the Ever-increasing wedding market, yet there is hardly any investment on quality information that prepares the couple, especially women, for what to expect.

By writing this book, Gurmit Kaur has fulfilled a need and a large gap in helping young girls prepare emotionally for the Sikh wedding. The book is a pioneering work that comprises real life experiences through case studies, and offers guidance through recommendations and tips. It's a voice of experience that cares, is protective, and speaks with an air of openness and honesty. Written in a conversational style, this book will be an interest to all those preparing to get married, their families, social scientists, and members of the general public. It is something that we can all relate to. It's a book that everyone should have on their book shelf to read, to reflect, and to act on I am indeed honoured to write this Foreword, and I pray that the light of Guru guide Gurmit's work evermore so that she can continue to inspire us.

Harminder Kaur (Executive Officer)
Community Education Academy
of Leadership (CEAL)

Build Strong Foundations in Life
Just like a Tree
Then Blossom Forth In Beauty
                    Gurmit Kaur

TABLE OF CONTENTS

Foreword 4
Introduction 8
Background of Asian Communities in the West ... 14
The Preparation 26
Building Trust With Your New Family 36
Your True Husband 43
Extended Asian Families 49
Understanding and Dealing With Difficult Mother-
   In-Laws 56
Developing Resilience 71
The Wedding Day 84
Resources and Support 94
Massis Blessing To You 97

INTRODUCTION

Why a book just for girls? Because, it is generally women, rather than men, who have to adjust and make dramatic changes when they marry. Women leave their families and have to adjust to a new life within a wider, extended Asian family.

This book has been inspired by my own experiences, as well as observations of other women's struggle to adjust to the extended Asian family. I was highly educated at a top British university. I worked hard, despite all odds, to obtain an education with little support other than personal ambition. I worked with commitment and dedication because of my determination to excel in my chosen field. However, I learned that in both professional and personal life, there are other success factors besides knowledge of one's field. In many instances, personalities clashed, thus creating unpleasant situations that became uncontrollable. Additionally, many women were complaining of similar experiences—that is, matters relating to partners and their struggle to live peacefully with Asian in-laws.

This problem is not only local, but also one of epic,

global proportion. The number of women who have struggled and even died as a result of entering into an Asian marriage is staggering. In India alone, since 2001 an estimated 100,000 women have been killed each year due to dowries. But the worrying factor is the increasing numbers of such deaths and dowry cases (BBC, 29 March 2014). Estimates suggest that approximately 25,000 women die because of dowry related causes, where parents are not economically well off, and therefore cannot afford to pay a dowry to the groom's family. Although the cause of this is not about being prepared for marriage, it can be perceived as sheer greed. A childhood dream destroyed, parents and siblings' lives broken, and another beautiful light lost to the cruel world. It is this world that we must prepare for. In the words of Judith Roden (NESTA, January 2015):

'If you prepare for anything, you can respond to anything'.

The central goal of this book is to support and enable you to feel comfortable in realizing your ambition of having and preserving your family. At least, that is every girl's childhood dream. The book is based on case studies, personal experience, and observations of what makes marriages work and what does not. My background is in research and management. However, I naively entered an arranged marriage, which only lasted a few weeks, but through this process, I learned so much. The whole experience was extremely difficult and totally changed my outlook on life.It also helped me empathize with others. When you have experienced difficulties and overcome them, you tend to be in better position to appreciate others in similar circumstances. Throughout my life, and with the support of none other than the Creator, I have managed to rebuild my life, career, and family. I overcame difficulty by relying on the Creator for support. The Developing Resilience section of this book details primarily my own support mechanism that I have used to get through life's challenges without resorting to needless harmful substances (which can be addictive).

The final section goes through the Sikh wedding ceremony. This marks the end of preparation and the beginning of a new life. This life can be beautiful and blissful if we prepare for the day. Our next life away from our mortal bodies depends on how much preparation we take to make it blissful. So too we must prepare carefully for life as wedded couples within the family. In Sikhi, the family life—being able to co-exist within the family—is regarded as the highest form of living in society.

However, life does not always go according to plan. Personalities and domestic politics, along with failure to adjust to the new Asian family structure, can prevent one's childhood dreams from becoming a reality. I have seen many families save all their lives to get their daughter married. They sacrificed many pleasures for that one day in their daughter's life, only to be emotionally broken when such dreams went unfilled. My motivation in writing this book is to help women understand the need to adjust to a new Asian community family structure, as well as to develop emotional resilience. whilst preparing for a future, but successful marriage life.

This book does not cover the cultural aspects of marriage, nor will it be a support towards understanding individual relationships with one's husband. However, it will cover the spiritual side of marriage. It makes the assumption that you will live with an extended family for a temporary period who will attempt to support you in dealing with the trials and tribulations of marriage in the first stage, when everything is apparently fresh or new. Many people find the first year of marriage the most difficult, and this is the time when most problems occur. Once the first year is over, you tend to slowly gain more control because of your increasing awareness of how to deal with this type of life. You will then build your own mechanisms with the aim of understanding the manner in which to cope with the complex issues of matrimonial union, and, more so, the novelty of marriage itself.

Hopefully, this book will give you some insight into preparing for your big day, as well as ideas about how to deal with some of the issues that you may face as a married woman. However, like other writings on marriage, this book has its limitations. For instance, I have not covered issues of forced marriages, homicidal in-laws, and abuse within the extended Asian family. These are widespread issues, but the intention of this book is to provide a positive, encouraging outlook on a very difficult and emotional subject. There are books written by women in which they have shared bitter experiences, but in the process of doing so, they are perceived as somewhat dishonouring their communities. Nevertheless, as an integral part of the Sikh community, my faith has given me a sense of belonging, though the journey has been difficult. I have developed various resilience strategies to remain within the community and, equally, to preserve with my faith, despite occasionally having the desire to opt out altogether. Whilst we may have failings in our community, we also have positive aspects, and it is against such a background that I have tried to maintain an optimistic outlook.

'Like the Poppy, they are dyed in the deep crimson colour of Truthfulness'
Guru Nanak Dev JI

BACKGROUND OF ASIAN COMMUNITIES IN THE WEST

Many Asian women are well educated and work hard in their careers, but they are not adequately prepared to live with their Asian in-laws or even within the wider Asian community. The lifestyle of third-generation Asian females is largely alien to the first- and second-generation Asians, and in many cases, third-generation families may be treated with hostility. The belief system of third-generation Asian females is likely to be different from first- and second-generation families, and many women may feel that they are entering the medieval era when they move in with their with in-laws. They are unable to deal with the constraints of personal and professional freedom. However, with knowledge and preparation, they should be able to adjust and thrive within the new family structure. Women should invest in preparing for this adjustment rather than investing thousands in their physical appearance on the actual wedding day. The Asian wedding market is worth £12 billion a year, which is more than twice as much as the UK's traditional

wedding market total of £5.5 billion, and this is a figure that is growing by 25% each year.
(http://asianlite.com/news/uk-news/rise-in-multicultural-brides-in-britain/)

When my sisters weremarried in the 1980s, the wedding costs were under £10,000. This figure has been bolstered by market increases, but also because there are more families who have successful, well-established businesses with greater disposable income. Upper-middle class families can sometimes spend over £70k on their daughter's wedding. The wedding scene has become very competitive amongst people, as they yearn to do better and stand out from the crowd. The focus on weddings has moved toward the actual ceremony, instead of emphasizing moral virtues and the determination needed to survive the challenges of marriage itself.

There was a mass migration of Asian men in the mid-1950s to rebuild Britain after World War II. They were invited to undertake the jobs that the indigenous population was unprepared to do. Most of the men worked in industry. For example, in the Midlands they found work in the steel and manufacturing sector. In West London, many found work in the airports and other industrial entities, while in the Northwest, others were employed in the textile industries. They came largely from village backgrounds and worked hard. Many did not seek entertainment in the West but were keen to preserve their faith and culture. So, in addition to working hard, they built

Gurdwaras, which meant that their social life revolved around these places of worship. In the 1960s and 1970s, many brought over their families, and settled into the Britain.

Village life was relatively straightforward for women; there were strict demarcations of roles. They stayed at home and looked after the family, while men worked outside of the home. Women supported each other and kept each other company as they undertook household duties. Their primary duties were to look after the family and community. Many endured hardships, but they focused on building a better life for their children. In terms of education, many were encouraged to pursue careers in vocational fields.

The second generation of workers entered higher education in large numbers and succeeded in entering fields such as medicine, accounting, and teaching. Many third-generation Sikhs are entering the arts and have become successful artists both in their own culture as well as in mainstream society.

However, the roles and responsibilities of third-generation Sikh women have changed dramatically over the past 30 years. They are no longer expected to stay at home and tend to family and community. They now have equal responsibilities for buying property and contributing to the costs of weddings. Their overall function as women within a family setting has tripled and so have the costs of weddings, with new industries having been established just to cater to this burgeoning Asian social festivity market. Wedding events are held in most major cities in the UK and around the globe. Banqueting halls are mushrooming in all major cities and towns.

These events last for days and weeks, but the commitment to marriage is one that should last a lifetime and that should not be taken lightly. We have the power to shape our lives as successful beings within our marriages in the Asian community while also keeping our careers intact. We have to develop emotional resilience and strength to deal with the new challenges that face us as wives, daughters-in-law, sisters-in-law, and the many other new roles that we will have to adopt.

Many women are increasingly achieving higher education degrees, and Asian females are excelling in a variety of fields, from aeronautical engineering to medicine. In fact, I once attended a bike show in the Birmingham Exhibition centre. There were two shows happening simultaneously: one aimed at the pharmaceutical industry and the other aimed at leisure cycling. Participants attending the pharmaceutical exhibition were of Asian background,while most of the attendees at the cycling showwere from indigenous white families. The first generation of the Asian community came into the country and worked primarily in industrial sectors. However, they encouraged their children to work in highly vocational sectors, where jobs were based on education rather than social networking. Therefore, a large number of second-generation Asians work in IT and medicine, as well as the financial and accounting sectors, all of which provide them with large disposable incomes. However, although Asians have worked hard in the vocational sectors, there are still only a few creative fields in which income for high-achievers remains patchy and competitive.

There was a time in the Sikh community when men and women did not meet or talk to each other prior to marriage. They met on the day of marriage, according to clearly defined rules. They were kept largely separate from each other. Many first and second women did work in the industrial, manufacturing and service sectors. Families lived as extended units, so there was little pressure for couples to buy a house. Women generally supported each other and looked after their husbands and children, but they also found joy in each other's company. I visited a local Sikh day centre full of elderly Sikh women. I wanted to ask them about their experiences of marriage and life. Were they nervous when they married a complete stranger and moved in with a strange family? The majority of female elders said they entrusted their parents with the right decision to find a suitor for them. They were happy, having lived joyous, satisfactory lives.

Practically all of these women praised their mothers-in-law and referred to the support they received from their seniors. They too gave comfort to their daughters-in-law, something I clearly did not expect to hear. Why? My Western mind was unable to comprehend someone marrying a complete stranger and being content with doing mundane work. Yet, for these women, there was little pretence.For their age, they looked young and appeared cheerful and fun-loving. From all appearances, these elderly women seemed to have none of the pressures and stresses that we tend to associate with household chores. Nor did they have to research in-laws; they had a network of women supporting each other, and they were content with few material gains. They met often to read Sukhmani Sahib and sang together to help cope with daily stresses. Singing together creates a sense of unity and peace. Women singing shabads together and being in the presence of the Guru Granth Sahib removes negative thoughts and anxieties; essentially, it builds resilience and strength.

Ladies listening to Sukhmani Sahib Prayers

There is little opportunity to do this today, as families are dispersed and/or largely isolated, often with both parents working to earn a living. However, matters pertaining to South Asian culture, including marriage and related subjects, are virtually accessible or available via the new Information Age. DVDs, the Internet, Podcasts, and iPhones can be utilized to remain connected with the Gurbani and, therefore, the all-pervading Almighty being.

Mutual Understanding

Before we enter any contractual relationship, including marriage, we must be sure that everything 'fits' and that we agree to the necessary arrangements, in order to reduce the likelihood of future shocks and unexpected decisions. To marry purely on the basis of attraction is both ungrounded and dangerous. Attraction can very quickly dissipate when there is a clash of cultures or personalities. It is advisable to marry someone with whom you have a common background and shared cultural understanding. This will ensure that despite challenges, you will continue with the matrimonial union because you have a common bond that will sustain you through the difficult times. This common bond should be faith or a series of shared interests that help you grow together within the relationship. This will avoid problems later on and help you to adjust more easily.

However, more importantly, it is absolutely necessary for you to discuss marriage with your parents. They want the best for your future. Sometimes, young people get married to satisfy their parents, and parents marry their children because they think they know what is best for young people. Honest and clear communication with parents is absolutely necessary for young women who are thinking of marriage. They must have the courage to talk to their parents about married life and to seek their advice about how to adjust to different circumstances and situations. We are not often taught how or even when to discuss personal issues, including matrimony, until it is too late.

CASE STUDY A: PREETI KAUR AGE 34

Preeti was a very much loved, innocent young lady who had successfully completed a University degree. She was very keen to please her parents and had never had a boyfriend during her student years. She knew little about male relationships and yet entered blindly into marriage. She went through the usual marital rituals, but she felt numb and disappointed by her decision. She did not know how to say "No" to her parents. Since her intention was to be the 'dutiful' daughter, she felt that she had no control over the situation. After the wedding, she felt rather uncomfortable and wanted to leave the matrimonial home. But, she could not convince her husband. She tried everything from having tantrums and crying, to eventually being abusive to her in-laws. She remained in the union for around 8 years, but she became extremely depressed, angry and ill. Her husband did not want to make a big financial commitment with someone who was mentally stressed, so they separated and eventually divorced. In hindsight, she felt that she did not have a sense of 'self' and did not feel she was (enough) of a mature adult to cope with the responsibilities of marriage.

Subsequently, Preeti's parents said that if she did not want to marry, she should have said so!

They got her married because they felt that it was what she wanted.

TALK TO YOUR PARENTS
In Asian communities, young girls rarely talk to their parents about relationships, marriage, and what it means to be married. Also, they infrequently discuss the changes and personal expectations that come with marriage, or whether or not the girl is ready to adapt tothis new way of life. As young women educate themselves, they open their minds to a whole new world of possibilities and ambitions. Every so often, if the mind so wishes and circumstances allow, these can be fulfilled. But very often, these can only be accomplished with adequate support from family members.

Talking to your parents about marital relations can be hard, but once you initiate the action, they'll understand and generally support you fully in the whole process.

SUMMARY POINTS AND REFLECTION

- Are you ready to commit to marriage for a lifetime?
- Do you feel you have the emotional resilience to cope with multiple roles and manage work simultaneously?
- Do you have the understanding and strength to cope with working and undertaking household duties?
- Do you know what financial commitments you will be expected to contribute toward your home?
- Have you identified trusted support mechanisms to help you cope with your new roles and responsibilities?
- Are you happy with everything in the arrangement? If not, can you identify areas of unhappiness or discomfort? Are you able to discuss these issues with your parents?
- Do you really want to get married? Do you feel that you have ambitions that will remain unfilled if and when you get married?
- Empathy is important in any relationship, whether we believe it or not, especially when entering a Sikh marriage - we are marrying into an extended family. We must remember that at one time, the mother in law (MIL) was a daughter in law (DIL). That as a senior female, she also yearns for friendship and respect of another woman who will share the rest of her life with. Invest in time to build a relationship with your mother in law, it will pay numerous

dividends for both family and community happiness.

Empathy is important in any relationship—whether we believe it or not—but it is especially important when entering a Sikh marriage, because we are marrying into an extended family. We must remember that, atone time, the mother-in-law (MIL) was a daughter-in-law (DIL). Also, as a senior female, she yearns for the friendship and respect of another woman who she will share the rest of her life with. Invest time in building a relationship with your mother-in-law; it will pay numerous dividends for all concerned.

"Let this mind of thine become the humming black-be and God's feet be the lotus flower".
                    Guru Arjan Dev Ji

THE PREPARATION

Your Husband on Earth

'She who gives her love to a passing traveller will not have anything'
Guru Arjan Dev Ji

Before marriage, it is important to know if the person you intend to spend your life with truly desires you. Your expected future prior to marriage may be the same after tying the nuptial knot. Thus, if the man you're courting makes no effort in your pre-marital relationship, it is unlikely that he will make any serious commitment thereafter. This, ofcourse, can be devastating after you marry, because you will need to work in partnership and make joint decisions together with your spouse. If he is unwilling to work with you, you may need to reconsider marriage in order to avoid unnecessary pain and hurt later. Observe patterns of behaviour, as these are unlikely to change over the long term. Think about whether you want your children to inherit these characteristics as well. Your future husband will also be the primary role model for your children.

There is a theory in a very popular book titled 'The Rules' by Ellen Fein and Sherrie Schneider (January 2007). This theory states that women should not chase men or initiate communication in intimate relationships. Women who are seen as clingy and needy are generally unattractive to men. Men are inherently and naturally the hunters; it is fundamental to their (human) nature. They enjoy pursuing, and if they are interested in you, then they will do so with immense pleasure. If they do not want you, then they will make no effort with you. In this case, you will need to seriously reconsider your decision.

This is a very important concept in Sikhi. We are not beggars. If we beg, we only beg for the support to meditate on Waheguru.

This is only theory, but there are other principles regarding love and relationships. Since it is still taboo for men and women to socialise in public, males are often unaware of, or, in other instances, don't how to interact with women, frequently finding it difficult to articulate feelings of affection. In this case, it is important to try and understand such sentiments, while simultaneously encouraging men so that they can effectively fulfil their duties in the long term.

In modern times, relationships can be complex and demanding because of the stressful lives we live. However, if we desire fulfilling lives, efforts must be made to accomplish our dreams.

CASE STUDY C: DISPY AGED 24

Dispy stayed in the company of girls at University and was perfectly happy with them. Every Valentine's Day the girls would exchange cards. They never socialized with boys and were satisfied with each other's company. All of the girls were strict Hindus and were never allowed to venture out. They studied and met at cafes ona weekly basis. When their studies were completed, they were ill equipped to deal with the realities of life, particularly marriage life within Asian households. Dispy had very little knowledge of elderly Asian women, such as what to do and how to behave around them, since that she had no previous relationship. She did not know what to expect, and so, when introduced to a young man at the local temple for the first time, she agreed to marry him. Her parents knew she was vulnerable, but her future mother-in-law kept insisting and pestering until the boy saw her. Even though she never went out with him, she built up an imageryof love. She began to fall in love. He never made any effort within the relationship; he never rang her, never wanted to meet up. In effect, he was not genuinely interested in her. Dispy felt unhappy and unwanted. She managed to get him to come spend the day out with her, but he made her pay for the coach trip, entrance fare, and even his ridehome. Then, he had the audacity to criticize her fashion sense. She had doubts about him and his love for her. But everyone at the temple knew of the wedding, and she felt pressured to marry him. They married, and she found out that his behaviour changed little. There was a time when she was at her parents' house and had left a coat at her in-laws. She requested that they meet in town where they both went to work and he could hand the coat over, as it was winter. He refused; he did not want to be seen with her without his parents' permission. He felt that every encounter of theirs had to be endorsed by his parents. His behaviour before marriage showed the same indifference to her needs as in the actual marriage. Nevertheless, she returned to her parents, and they refused to allow her to return to the husband out of fear of further abuse. They divorced.

RESEARCH

It is advisable to get to know your future in-laws as much as you possibly can. Your future in-laws will greet you with love and warmth, reciprocate this affection. Understand that we are all human beings, and your in-laws will be just as nervous as you especially if its their first born getting married. They too will be unsure about you and your likes and dislikes. The simple benefits of smiling and showing that you care will break down many barriers. Remember affection begets affection, respect begets respect. What you want to do on the onset is to build a lasting relationship based on mutual respect. The traditional daughter in law is expected to be obedient and venerate her in-laws. The 21st daughter in law has a voice and a strong one too. Use your voice wisely. Remember treat people as you would like to be treated yourself. A good start would be make the effort to find out what they like; every family culture has its own likes and dislikes.

If possible gain an understanding or some knowledge prior to entering into your marriage life. You may not share all of your interests with your future in laws but keep an open mind and be prepared to compromise or develop common interests. Also, if you feel unable to fit into the family structure or if the family is secretive about their family life, try to explore the reason for such attitudes. Will they want to keep you in the kitchen and restrict your freedom? If they are hiding from you or do not want to have any contact with you before the marriage, then they are likely to be highly conservative in their traditional values about women, including their place in family and society. Again, the same rule applies to your in-laws if you are to live with them. If they make little or no effort to show dignity and respect toward you, as well as to accommodate your initial needs, then after marriage, it is unlikely that they will make any effort to cater to your needs and wants.

Asian men have been brought up with a deep-rooted attachment to their parents and the support they provide. Never underestimate this type of bond between men and their families. Your relationship might be deeply affected if there are conflicts between you and your husband's family. Many marriages have disintegrated due to disagreements, often based on a clear lack of love, appreciation, respect, and understanding. Saying unkind words to your in-laws can cause permanent damage to your marriage. Always remember the simple rule:

'That soul-bride, who talks sweetly and speaks the Truth, O Siblings of Destiny, becomes pleasing to her Husband Lord'
Guru Nanak Dev Ji.

As a woman, there is also the risk of violence, which may be due to existing tensions. Men may find it difficult to talk about their emotions, and instead tend to express frustration and anger towards women because of a lack of support in dealing with troubled or challenging family situations. His way of resolving it is 'to put you in your place', since he expects you to conform to his parents bidding, that is, their customs and traditions of 'doing things'. It is often said that the first year of marriage can be both testing and challenging as two individuals adjust to one another, understand thought processes and learn about each other ways of handling life's success and challenges. The saying 'those who pray together stay together' is befitting to the Sikh way of life.

One particular emotion that is important to severis one's ego and alter-ego, especially if you are desirous of a successful marriage. The self is no longer the self; you will be with your husband for the rest of your life. Souls do not blend where ego rules the hearts and minds, youwill need to remove barriers that may prevent the stability ofyour marital union. You will need to find someone with whom you are emotionally and socially compatible, as this makes the marriage less challenging over the long term and is thus a vital factor for a successful marriage.

Most girls are given the opportunity to study and develop while they are living with their parents. However, this changes when they become daughters-in-law. You will be expected to equally share household duties. Initially, this may be a shock to the system, but eventually you will learn to take it in stride. Marriage in many ways is like yoga. Yoga means to break the self and join with the universe. As a married woman, you will have to let go of yourself and join with your in-laws. Before you join with your in-laws, it is important that you share some if not all values as them.

In the days of arranged marriages, parents chose couples from compatible families. The idea was to ensure the possibility of greater amicable relations within both families. This was often based on community trust and word-of-mouth from relatives. However, this tradition has largelydisappeared,as young people are now expected to find suitable partners while maintaining the traditions of living with in-laws. In addition to this, marriage rituals are still very traditional despite the many changes in society. Because many couples have to stay with their in-laws longer nowadays (since, for instance, it may take longer to save up for a home in a burgeoning property market), it's even more important to understand and live peacefully with one another.

Many Sikh girls feel strongly obligated to satisfy their parents' wishes. The community in which we live places a strong emphasis on social values as opposed to individual needs and desires. We live in a community and socialize within it. The Gurdwara structure requires community volunteers to make it work and thrive. However, girls can get carried away with trying to 'please' everyone except themselves. They repress their own needs and desires, as well as the freedom to explore the world and understand where they fit in. This desire is not extinguished after marriage, and it can destroy your in-laws' family as well as your own.

However, third-generation Sikh women are less inclined toward community values since individual aspirations have become more important to them in modern times. This causes a clash of cultures within the family when they enter their husband's household. However, girls must understand that they need to adapt to the new family culture, similar to the way they adjust to corporate lifestyles when they go to work. It is important to recognise that such a process takes time. Patience, therefore, is the key in all of this.

MASSI'S SUMMARY POINTS AND REFLECTION
- If he makes no effort in your relationship before marriage, he will not make any effort afterward.
- Observe and note patterns of behaviour and general attitudes.
- Do you want your children to inherit these negative behaviours?
- Remember, if he does not want you, he will make no effort with you. Asian girls who have been denied love and attention by

their fathers will attempt to recreate or relive the same experience and relationship with future partners. Are you in a union where your partner makes no effort to nourish the relationship?
- Do you feel that your love is not returned? If you are spurned or jilted and there are unreasonable patterns of behaviour then cancel the wedding because nothing will change afterward.

Just as the Meerkat looks after her family, know that mother earth is looking after you always.
Gurmit Kaur

BUILDING TRUST WITH YOUR NEW FAMILY

In modern times, we must learn to develop the skills to navigate not only the web, but also Asian culture. This means learning to successfully protect yourself. You are a precious being, and many people will depend on you to give and receive love. You have a childhood dream of having your own cosy little family, but only by looking after yourself can you achieve your dream. Look after yourself both physically and mentally.

Be cautious with who you discuss your problems with and refrain from gossiping with anyone. Gossip always returns and can exacerbate situations with irreversible consequences for you and others. The damage and loss of trust can also be irreparable. If you must talk to your parents, then find a practical way to resolve the situation with them, but do not include your husband in such discussions. However, do not involve your parents with his parents, since this can lead to deep distrust with your in-laws. You have to solve intimate marriage problems independently and learn how to manage issues in relationships like an adult.

(This does not apply to physical abuse within families; in this case, seek support and look after yourself.) For the first few months, make your observations, just as you observe you too will be observed. The first few months of marriage can be beautiful yet also the toughest to deal with for any couple. However, in Asian marriages, we have the additional responsibilities of coping with living with our in-laws. See it in a positive light and work towards a lasting relationship.

> ### *CASE STUDY D: SONIA AGED 32*
> Sonia had known her in-laws all her life; they were close family friends. Sonia was an only child, and both sets of parents were desirous of their children being married. There was much trust and love within the families, and they had helped each other for a year. Sonia and her fiancé went out as teenagers and then through University. She knew her mother-in-law well. She was very friendly at the Gurdwara and always greeted her warmly. The couple married and everything was going well, until she had an argument with her husband. Her in-laws overheard the misunderstanding and started distancing themselves from her and not speaking to her for weeks. Her in-laws chose to support her husband, and this created a further rift between the couple. She found it difficult to maintain a normal relationship with her husband and confided in her parents. They visited and tried to help resolve the situation on numerous occasions but to no avail. Sonia was determined for the marriage to work and applied herself diligently to various domestic chores, but she felt

that such efforts weren't enough. She felt more like the family's housekeeper than a part of the household. Her mother-in-law changed her behaviour towards her and rather than support her, neglected her and resorted to superstitious activities. Eventually, after years of trying, her husband told her that he did not want her anymore.

NEVER TALK ABOUT YOUR IN-LAWS
This book will not cover relationship issues between couples, but we have to bear in mind that the first year or two is important. It is during those first years that trust has to be built between the couple, rather than discussing marital problems with parents.

Your own parents gave you birth, nurtured you, taught you skills, protected you, supported you through 'thick and thin'. They will always remain your biological parents. Your parents in law on the other hand too will be as protective, as loving and as supportive of you. Of course this will depend on each individual family too. If they are loving towards you, reciprocate the same. This will help to develop a strong bond between you and your 'new' parents. The nurturing of this relationship means that your children will forever remain grateful for. All children love their grandparents and a beautiful legacy to pass onto the children is a stable relationship with both your own parents as well as the parents of your husband. Acceptance is the key for both parties.

There will be times when your husband shows little interest in the marital relationship. Do not pester him, but rather seek your own pleasures. There are many things to do to compensate for lack of attention. Men sometimes need space and cannot articulate their feelings; you might feel neglected or that he is abandoning you. But very often, this is not the case. Use this opportunity to read Gurbani and invest in knowledge and spirituality. The creator of the Universe is your spiritual husband. Never seek the company of other men or other harmful addictions to fill the loneliness gap in your life. Remember first and foremost who your real husband is.

There will be times when your husband fails to give you attention. It is in those times that we must remember who our spiritual and real husband is. He is the Creator of all. He is without fear, and when no one else supports you, He will be your support. If the problem within the family is an issue of violence, there are support groups who will support you and protect you (a list of them can be found at the back of this book)

But if there are otherdistressing issues then speak with a trusted friend or trusted member of the family who can help to guide you or help you to problem solve. Most important factor. Your in-law family wants to be able to trust you with all of the problems within the family. All families have issues and problems, and by building trust, many of these can be resolved. In the end, there are more of them than you, and there will be personality clashes; it is not easy. But it is in those very times that you must pray and build your inner strength.

Seek the support of a greater force from the Creator, There is no greater forcethan the Love from the Creator.

My own son was 7 years old when he first started Punjabi class. For the first few months of class, he did nothing except observe.He did not misbehave; he just sat there and refused to do anything. His teacher complained that he just sat there, but there was nothing I could do. I was just grateful that he attended and was in a Punjabi learning environment; it was a good sign, especially for his future. At least he was listening and absorbing aspects of spirituality and his ancestral roots. Over a year later, he wrote love letters to his dad in Punjabi. I can barely write it myself! He enjoys going to class, but he **needed time to absorb, trust, and understand. He wanted to assess the overall picture, and he learned well.**

Seek to learn the culture of the family, possibly before you get married. Understand how they work and where you fit in. Remember your childhood dream of having your own house, children, and a loving husband. That is your goal, and just as you worked hard to learn and achieve in your chosen career, you must also apply this to your personal life. Learn the culture and values of your new family. If you cannot do this, ask your mother and aunts about how they fit in and how they dealt with certain situations. Aunties are always willing to share their experiences. There is nothing that aunties like to do better than to share their experiences. Listen and learn about your auntie's experience; equip yourself with the knowledge to navigate between the two cultures. You will be rewarded.

Summary Points
- Resist the temptation to gossip or say ill things about your in-laws' to other family members. If you have to talk to someone, then do so with a trusted female friend who is not part of the extended in-law family.
- Learn the culture of the family before you marry and learn to bridge the gap between the two generations.

Without you Lord I am incomplete
*****Gurmit Kaur*****

YOUR TRUE HUSBAND

'God is your Husband: He is Handsome and True, He is obtained by reflecting upon the Guru'
Guru Amar Daas Ji

Every girl has a dream that one day she will be married and that everyone will delight in her beauty and clothes. You dream of meeting a man who will adore and love you every day for the rest of your life. You will have lovely children, whom you will delightfully look after.

This dream can come true, and your wishes can come true. However, like everything else, to obtain your wishes, you will have to learn. The very word Sikhi means learning; we are always learning. We are learning to prepare to enter our in-laws' house. Sikhs are essentially all brides, both male and female. Through our lives on this earth, we are essentially being prepared to enter our next life, which is with the Creator. Who is our true husband?

'God is your Husband, He is Handsome and True, He is obtained by reflecting upon the Guru'
Guru Amas Dev Ji

This applies to both men and women; too much emotional attachment to earthly affairs is generally discouraged in Sikhi. Throughout life you will go through many ups and downs. Life can be very demanding, but detachment is the key to seeing things through. For example, like the heart beat on the monitor goes up and down, so does life. But,there is a straight line where there are no ups and downs; it is just straight. Your aim is to be like the straight line, but alive and existing within the family and community. Although, being too attached to them is also not good.

'Gazing upon their families, people are lured and trapped by emotional attachment but none will go with them in the end'.
Guru Nanak Dev Ji

As a female, you will be the strength and foundation of your in-laws' family. Every group has an innate desire to sustain themselves and continue to survive. Never underestimate your role within the family because it is very powerful. Every word you say has multiple implications as you enter your in-laws' household. While you were at your parents' home, you had the luxury to do as you pleased, within reason. No one really bothered you; you were forgiven because you were the daughter of the house. However, when you enter your in-laws' home, you are a stranger. They will be wary of you because of the impact of your presence on their overall lives. So, in every instance, talk sweetly:

'That soul-bride, who talks sweetly and speaks the Truth, O Siblings of Destiny, becomes pleasing to her Husband Lord'.
Guru Nanak Dev Ji

You can start by learning this habit in your parents' home. The investment you make learning these things will pay multiple dividends in the end for your future and may save you from a broken heart. Your husband wants you to show equal respect to his parents and other family relatives as well. Everyone wants to be loved forever; showing love to his family, elders, and children means that you will receive affection from them as well. The elderly and children demand, often cry, for love. If you are in an extended family with a number of elders and children, you will find that your responsibilities, including emotional relationships, will increase. However, there is a danger of burnout syndrome, as doing menial or repetitive routine household tasks can take their toll, especially when you thought you were just marrying your husband but end up having an intense relationship with his grandma and his sister's or brother's kids. Do set boundaries to protect yourself. Offer some of your time and love, but do set limits if you are working as well. You will need energy for work and other duties.

You need to ensure that you maintain your health and preserve your general well-being in such a new social environment. Most importantly, nourishing your relationship with your husband should always take priority. However, you must also nourish your relationship with the Creator of Life, Waheguru. Remember your marriage vows when you grasp the hem of His robe. We will discuss this in greater detail in the Wedding Day section. Your true husband is the Creator of this world.

Summary Points
- Obtain strength from our True Guru.
- Remember your True Husband is the Creator Lord.
- Do not get attached to your extended family. In the end, no one will accompany you.
- Watch your words, because they can have multiple implications.
- Set boundaries at the beginning; you cannot cater to everyone's needs.
- Look after yourself and nourish the relationship you have with the Creator Lord.
- At the very beginning, get to know your in-laws and treat them with great dignity, respect, and warmth.
- Discover the likes and dislikes of your in-laws. Remember, you will be staying with them, possibly on a temporary basis, and you must make every effort to reassure them of your honesty and purpose within the new family circle.
- If they refuse to allow you to get to know them, they are possibly very conservative; therefore, they will expect traditional roles for women. Are you willing and prepared for this?

- Never underestimate the bond between boys/men and their parents. Never ever say anything to upset your in-laws.
- Are you prepared to give a part of your mind, body, and soul to your husband? To be truly successful, you will need to do this. To blend successfully, compatibility with your husband is necessary.

Be connected with everyone but belong to none
Gurmit Kaur

EXTENDED ASIAN FAMILIES

'If the One God be my friend, all will be my friends, if the One God be my enemy everyone will quarrel with me'
Guru Arjan Dev Ji

When we enter Asian marriages overnight, our roles in society and the expectations placed upon us multiply. From being a single woman to an auntie, daughter-in-law, and wife can be overwhelming, if not daunting, especially if you have been brought up in the West, where the principles of individuality and independence are highly valued. Generally, Asian families are a community within themselves. Of particular importance is the Milni. In Sikh marriages, you are not just marrying the husband; your family will be wedded to his family. Therefore, there is a formal introduction of your relatives to his relatives, starting with the eldest relative and then the youngest. The male and female Milni are separated, and there is an exchange of gifts from the bride's side to the bridegroom's side. However, there has been a new trend of having the male and female Milni together during this event. The role of the Milni in Sikh culture or Faith needs more in-depth research by social scientists and other leaders. The exchange of gifts acts as a sweetener to the bridegroom's family, encouraging them to treat the new bride with love because she is a new bridge that will need the affection of the wider extended family. In light of the extended families' marriage to one another, we must first of all understand special names that are integral to our cultural heritage.

For example, your dad's sister is your bhuaji, and not merely an aunt, or your mom's sister is your massi, and not merely an aunt. There is etymology at play here. South Asian languages are very rich; there is a word for every nuance and a relation too. Using the proper names also helps to establish who is who. The following is a list of relatives' names you should be aware of and possibly memorise before the wedding:

Mother – Mataji
Father – Papaji
Son – Putar
Daughter – Dhee
My Mother's Mother – Naniji
My Mother's Father – Nanaji
My Father's Mother – Dadiji
My Father's Father – Dadaji
My Older Brother – Veerji
My Younger Brother – Kaka
My Sister – Bhenji
My Younger Sister – Bhen
My Mother's Grandparents – Parnani / Parnana
My Father's Grandparents - Pardadi / Pardada

My Husband – Gharwala (loosely translated: Man of the House)
My Wife – Wohti (loosely translated: Bride)
My Father's Older Brother – Taya
My Father's Older Brother's Wife -Tayee
My Father's Younger Brother -Chacha
My Father's Younger Brother's Wife - Chachi
My Father's Sister - Bhua
My Father's Sister's Husband – Phupher
My Mother's Brother - Mama
My Mother's Brother's Wife - Mami
My Mother's Sister – Masi
My Mother's Sister's Husband – Masar
My Brother's Wife – Bharjayee or Bhabi
My Brother's Son – Bhateeja
My Brother's Daughter – Bhateejee
My Sister's Husband - Jeeeja
My Sister's Son - Panewa or Bhanja
My Sister's Daughter – Panewee
My Wife's Brother – Sala (but you never say Salaji!)
My Wife's Brother's Wife – Salehar
My Wife's Sister – Sali
My Wife's Sister's Husband – Sandhu
My Husband's Sister – Nanaan
My Husband's Sister's Husband – NanaanWaya
My Husband's Older Brother – Jeth
My Husband's Older Brother's Wife – Jethani
My Husband's Younger Brother – Dewar
My Husband's Younger Brother's Wife – Dewarani
My Son's Son – Potra
My Son's Daughter – Potri
My Daughter's Son – Dotra
My Daughter's Daughter – Dotri

My Son-in-Law – Jawai
My Daughter-in-Law – Noo
My Father-in-Law – Sora
My Mother-in-Law – Sas
Father-in-Law to Father-in-Law – Kurm
Mother-in-Law to Mother-in-Law - Kurmani

Reference: http://kasaindian.com/indian-restaurant-sf/2009/05/the-extended-punjabi-family/

In the first few months, you may feel overwhelmed by the strangeness of carrying so many different titles, many of which you were previously unaware. However, soon you will learn about your husband's relatives and realise too that, despite their differences, they can be delightful company.

Generally, everyone will be excited to see and welcome the new member of the family to the house.

Your sisters-in-law could be your greatest ally or your greatest rivals in helping you settle in with your new family. If they offer words of advice, use your own judgment but their advice can be very useful simply because they have been through similar experiences.

Sometimes tensions can erupt between you and female relatives; for example, your husband's brother's wife or wives have probably been through difficulty in settling in also. She has either resented the changes she has had to make and wants to continue the same cycle, or she will be kind and support you in the process of making such essential changes. If she has successfully adapted to the family culture, she will be put on a pedestal. She might also be jealous because of losing the attention of others. Again, enter into the household carefully, with the intention of not upsetting anyone. Your sister-in-law can also be your greatest support and ally. In this case, nurture and invest time in learning from her how to adjust to the new family. Always listen to her advice, because she has experienced the processes of adjusting to new family settings and will be keen to support you.

When entering into a new household, the new bride must prepare. You can do this by learning about the family's behaviour. What are their likes and dislikes? Do they allow you to come and visit? If they do not, you will need to consider why not. The traditional custom was that girls rarely visited parents' home before marriage, but this custom has changed.If your in-laws adhere to traditional values before marriage, it is likely that they will be strictly obedient to such values after your marriage as well.

Summary Points
- Learn how to address extended family members. Avoid addressing them on first name terms; instead address them based on the relationship you have with them. For example, call your father-in-law, Daddy

Ji, or your sister-in-law, Bhabi Ji. Adding a Ji shows a sign of respect, and they will feel better if you pay homage to them.
- Seek the support of sisters-in-law; they will guide you in adjusting to the family culture.
- Endeavour to learn about the culture of the family before you enter it and prepare to adjust.
- If you are not inclined to adjust to the family or your husband, have the courage to say no. There are other families whose culture is similar to yours.

Live each day without fear, seek strength from the universe and creator.
Gurmit Kaur

UNDERSTANDING AND DEALING WITH DIFFICULT MOTHER-IN-LAWS

'O Nanak, one who understands His Command, does not speak in ego'
Guru Nanak Dev Ji

Generally, most mothers-in-law are friendly and supportive in accommodating your needs. My own mother-in-law longed for a daughter to care for and, therefore, she treated me like her daughter. She was a full-time housewife and used to cook lovely dishes for me every day. Her eyes used to sparkle every time I entered the Gurdwara. I remember always looking on my left, where she sat, just to see her eyes light up and enjoy the love and pride she had for me. Even at her funeral, I had momentarily forgotten the whole day and looked for her loving eyes. It had become a habit for me; one I was reluctant to give up. She died too early, but she gave me the most amazing love that one could ask for before moving on to abetter place.

Although my late mother-in-law was an angel and

welcomed me with a big heart, many still feel out of touch with the younger generation, not knowing how to relate to them. Some families tend to find younger people's lifestyles threatening, but generally they will try and support girls in their new roles.

If mothers-in-law are second generation South Asians or have worked most of their life in the West, they are less likely to expect their daughters-in-law to follow traditions; therefore, they will have fewer expectations. Mostly mothers-in-law are very excited to have a new daughter-in-law, and they desire a warm, close relationship with them.

> ### *CASE STUDY E: SANDY AGED 70*
> Sandy's own mother-in-law died before she got to know her, and when she married, she lived with her extended family. A first-generation Sikh, she was an educated health professional. She worked hard and had an arranged marriage. She had two boys and longed for a daughter to share her life with. When her son got married, she thought she had an opportunity to finally have a daughter. She visualized having a mother-daughter relationship with her daughter-in-law, as well as friendship. Sandy was very excited and looked forward to her daughter-in-law. She wanted to shower her with much love and affection, which she did. Unfortunately, the daughter-in-law did not reciprocate; instead, she showed little appreciation for Sandy's feelings or generosity of spirit.

Finally, her son got married, and after the wedding, her daughter-in-law came to the house. Sandy's husband loudly greeted the new daughter-in-law, 'Meet our princess – we have been waiting for you all our lives'. The family was overjoyed to have a daughter-in-law. Sandy used to come home after work and make tea for the family and cook. The daughter-in-law never once offered to help with the housework. When Sandy's dad died, she took her daughter-in-law to the hospital to see her him. Sandy was in a bad state and held onto her daughter-in-law tightly without realizing that she had never seen a dead body before. Sandy was very distressed and needed someone with her. One day while cleaning the bedroom, she found a Valentine's Day card with the words 'Hey babe, sorry you have to put up with my xxxxxx mum. One day I will make up for it'. Sandy was shocked. She thought her daughter-in-law was happy, and she had been very accommodating to her every need. She felt very hurt, but she forgave her and realized that she should not have taken her daughter-in-law to the hospital, as she was affected emotionally. After a few months, the couple moved out. Sandy still endeavours to accommodate her daughter-in-law, but when Sandy comes to visit, the daughter-in-law never cooks; instead, she expects her in-laws to take them out and pay for the meal.

CASE STUDY F: TANIA AGED 26

Tania had just finished University and was courting a young Sikh man who lived and worked in the city. Both sets of parents were Second-

> generation South Asians whose parents had been employed in the industrial sectors, but they had jobs in service industries and then ran businesses. As Tania's parents were working, Tania spent a lot of time with her grandmother, who taught her the proper etiquettes to live with her in-laws successfully. Tania knew she was entering an unknown zone, but she quickly made every effort to be pleasant while she learned about her new family. She showed respect to the elders by touching their feet. Although this surprised the family, who were also westernised, it was received well, since they understood that Tania was making efforts to fit into the family. After the initial touching of the elders'feet, she did not do this again, as it was not a part of her new family's culture. In the first year of marriage, she had very little contact with her own family.
>
> This caused her stress because she did not have employment, but she saw through it, and eventually things worked out for her. She is now successfully settled in her marriage and extended family.

The first year of marriage can be a challenge, and this is when you build foundations for the future. It is advisable in my experience to spend more time in learning about the new family and adjusting into the new house. Your parents would also want you to do the same. The experiences are similar to staying away from home. You are prone to home sickness especially in the first few months. Just as some students adapt to a new university setting easily for others it takes time. If you have anxieties, discuss them with your new family. They will then see you as someone who they can relate to and support. Most 21st century mother in laws will understand your anxiety, remember they too were daughter in laws once. It is also advisable to seek support from your new family, your new family will feel valued as you invest some form of trust in them. Building trust is most important during the first year of marriage.

Once this has been firmly established, you can work together to resolve all of the ups and downs of life within your new family.

The next section is about preparing yourself to deal with the difficulties of fitting in with mothers-in-law.

I have included a detailed section about how to deal with a difficult mother-in-law. Mothers-in-law play an important part in successful marriages. I have seen many unions fail because of a bride's inability to cooperate with her mother-in-law and vice versa. This topic is part of another section of this book. I have listed all of the difficult mother-in-law scenarios you could possibly face and explained how to deal with them using Gurbani.

DIFFICULT MOTHER-IN-LAWS
These are mothers-in-law (MILs) who crave all of the attention and feel the world revolves around them.

One advantage for the narcissistic mother-in-law who doesn't attend the wedding is that the attention will be diverted from her. She likes to be the centre of the family circle and the focus on the bride will cause her to be deeply upset. She acts overjoyed with relatives, but deep inside she is resentful because her matriarchal role is being challenged. She has a tough job ahead of her because she must show her daughter-in-law who is the boss and make her understand the 'culture' of the family. In many instances, she may have been a subject of abuse and is aware that her daughter-in-law must learn the obligation of preserving family kinship through honour, respect, and understanding. This is the cycle of male patriarchy, in which age-old traditions often clash with the values of modern-day Asian families. This does have an impact on women because they find it difficult to understand their roles and positions in the family within such a hierarchical structure. She has a very difficult task ahead of her to reshape the new woman of the family, which includes separating her from her family and friends so she can indoctrinate her into her new role.

This may and often will involve breaking the daughter-in-law's spirit and confidence.

The mother-in-law does so by constantly undermining her and looking for mistakes, or even invading her privacy.

Psychodynamic theory holds that every childhood

experience has a deep and lasting impact on the individual. Narcissism arises when parents are out of touch with their children's wishes. More often than not, Indian girls are seen as burdens, and their births are not celebrated. Girls are often malnourished in India, and their chances of survival are lessened due to neglect. This interferes with the ability to care for their well-being, thereby undermining their development of a sense of right and wrong. This neglect turns into trapped anger, and although they are keen to please their parents, their parents are disappointed that their girl is not a boy. The girl feels obliged to act out and develops traits that emphasize masculinity. In the process, she tends to downplay individual needs and desires in order to fulfil parental wishes and desires for a boy.

Case Study G: Pinkie Aged 28

Pinkie was the second daughter in a family that was desperate for a boy. Pinkie very often felt that her parents loved her older sibling more since they focused attention on her and supported her ambitions over Pinkie's. She felt very neglected and wanted to please her parents; the only way she felt she could do this was to supress her feminine feelings. She undertook a male-dominated degree and never dated boys. Opportunities to socialize with boys were limited. She had an arranged marriage, although she agreed to marry without dating the young man. The young man's older brother left his wife for a year and largely neglected her before moving out of the parents' house. Therefore, Pinkie's husband felt it was normal to neglect his wife too. His behaviour was very childish. Living with his parents and being looked after like a child, he behaved very much like a child after marriage. He did not take responsibility of caring for his wife. For him, paying attention to his wife would have gone against the family culture. This was a culture that largely differentiated the roles of men and women. This was acceptable in the older age, but with women pursuing degrees and jobs, such gender segregation is no longer feasible.

Women are expected to contribute financially, as well to handle the burden of household duties. The family culture took priority, and the continuation of the culture was paramount. The husband siding with his wife would mean that he was weak; he took every opportunity to show his alliance to his family. Her mother-in-law was constantly goading him (the husband) to show his wife that she was under his control, which was very much like a dictatorship.

The daughter-in-law had a difficult time settling in with her in-laws when she first got married. She stayed in an abusive marriage and made her children feel guilty and obliged to her. Her son's desire and need to please his mum was far more important than his desire to make his new wife happy. She was, in essence, a complete stranger in the house. The constant abuse broke her self-confidence; the burden of the housework expected of her also made her exhausted. She returned to her parents' house, but she did not want to end

> the marriage. Her mother-in-law started gossiping about Pinkie, and eventually her husband sent the divorce papers.

The MIL showed grandiose narcissistic features in dominating the family and her sons' marriages. This created a destructive outcome for both her sons and daughters-in-law, as well as her own Izzat.

She appeared outwardly over confident while devaluing her daughter-in-law in her attempt to protect her rather fragile self-esteem. MILs who are confident and have self-esteem do not need to abuse their daughters-in-law.

Coping with a narcissistic MIL is very stressful. Starting a job and then moving into a new family household can be very tough—emotionally, mentally, and physically. However, your attitude and actions can significantly affect your stress levels.

In this case, try to avoid attempting to change behaviour. It will not work in the Indian Family Hierarchy. You will only feel belittled, and further attempts at changing behaviour can lead to frustration. Try to find ways to repel negative behaviours, such as avoiding arguments or criticisms. These will irreversibly damage your relationship with your husband.

Bear in mind the strong bond that your husband has with his Mother, and understand that arguments will cause him profound distress. The odds are that he will side with his mother, the woman who has cared and provided for him since birth.

There are steps you can take to avoid problematic situations with your MIL. First, identify those situations and factors that lead to problems and avoid them whenever possible.

In order to survive the Narcissistic Mother-In-Law, you will have to exercise an unusual level of tact. Therefore, never criticize her, do not complain of unfairness, and definitely never point out your education, status,or savings. You are living inside their premises and under their rules. You will need to show loyalty to the family culture.

Show respect for your mother-in-law and support her fragile self-esteem. Do not show off in front of her. In the long term, when you have the opportunity, you will live away from your in-laws. It is safe for you as a daughter-in-law to take an interest in her life and show an admiration for all the hard work she has done to keep the family going. This will decrease any tensions.

Remember Guru Nanaks words in Jap Ji Sahib:

'O Nanak, one who understands His Command, does not speak in ego'
Guru Nanak Dev Ji

Never, ever display your superior status in terms of education and professionalism to your mother-in- law. This will only increase tension and difficulties; whenever possible, show only love and understanding.

A manipulative mother-in-law will observe every step you take and try to explain to you how to do everything, while expecting your absolute obedience. She will appear to be loving and sympathetic, wanting to support you in fitting in with her family's culture. Mothers-in-law have been through the process and want to help. Having a new member of the family can be quite overwhelming for them, and they might feel that their world is going to be confused and chaotic. They will attempt to control this by micromanaging their new daughter-in-law. They get a sense of power and satisfaction from being able to control your life and environment. Manipulative mothers-in-law share many characteristics with narcissistic mothers-in-law. They have limited empathy for others and will feel the need to control their daughter-in-law. They can be dangerous, because they will scrutinize and control your every moment in order to obtain absolute obedience.

If you are used to freedom and have grown up with parental love and support, you will find it difficult to tolerate most manipulators. Living with such persons can sap your energy, as you have to struggle to fit in with the family culture. Very often, the joy and pleasures of marriage are removed because you feel uneasy within the household.

Living with the manipulative mother-in-law can be very stressful, and the same rules as those used for the narcissistic MIL need to be applied. Its best not to show off, criticize,or point out mistakes. This will lead to further narcissism and a blind desire for personal attack. It is advisable also not to challenge her authority; maintain calm and serenity, while concentrating on saving to buy your new home.

As mentioned previously, look out for their traits before marriage and assess whether you are able to deal with them. Do not take their behaviour personally. You can support them in thinking that new ideas and the success of the family are due to their hard work and commitment.

Eventually, the mother-in-law will feel that you have acknowledged and respected her as her elder. This can result in her desire or appetite for less control over what you say or do. Although this may take months or even years, remember your long-term goal is to try and preserve the marriage so that you can have your dream house and family. Refrain from complaining about your mother-in-law to your husband. Constant complaining will cause him undue stress, leading to a damaged marital relationship.

Dealing with different types of difficult mother-in-laws:

The first step in coping with difficult mothers-in law is identifying what lies underneath the difficult and aggressive behaviour. Having a new person in your home may cause much fear and anxiety, and mothers-in-law tend to feel threatened, so they may react in an aggressive manner.

Different types of behaviour:

- **Frantic:** Help her to remain calm and understand your role in assisting with domestic chores.
- **Irritable:** Help her to solve problems and resolve conflicts; wait for the storm to pass. It will not last long.
- **Bullying:** Seek professional support.
- **Ruthlessness:** Help her understand the negative impact of her behaviour on the things she values and how changing her behaviour will benefit the family.
- **Passive- Aggressive:** Avoid any long discussions, which will only drain you and not bring you any benefits.

(A list of organizations that support women undergoing abusive relationships is available at theback of this book.)

We have examined some of the issues that are likely to occur and cause problems in a new family setting. This is not an exhaustive list. Many young people who struggle to purchase their own property and live with their in-laws can use this opportunity to save and buy their own property in the future. It makes both economic and social sense to learn how to adjust to your in-laws' home with faith in the Creator and universe that one day you will be able to purchase your own house.

MASSI'S SUMMARY POINTS
- Appreciate that you will be entering a new household and, therefore, need to build a strong foundation of love and trust with your in-laws.
- Try to avoid seeking support from your family in the first year and, if possible, have little contact with them as you adjust to your new family. This might seem harsh, but your overriding priority is to build foundations with your new family.
- Most mothers-in-law offer you a warm welcome, although there are some who will need understanding in the initial stages. Learn to deal with typical aggressive behaviours and develop coping strategies to manage family pressures, since they can make your life very stressful indeed.

When you connect with the Lord Our Creator
your foundations will be stronger
Gurmit Kaur

DEVELOPING RESILIENCE

This book has attempted to cover some of the challenges married women face. As we go through different stages in our matrimonial life, we have to contend with and learn to manage issues associated with married life. Preparing for some of these challenges will enable you to become a stronger person. However, as this is a new stage, later on you will need support. This book has dealt primarily with providing support via faith. From my own experience with battles in life, I have used my nature, breathing, and faith to help me cope and deal with all of life's issues.

Look after your heart:
South Asian women have a higher risk of heart disease than the indigenous Western population. I found that because of the issues that we have to deal with as women in the family and community, we are often expected to be tough and persevere in spite of health problems. It is in this process of hardening up that our hearts create blocks. Thus, there comes a time when our hearts are so blocked from coping with all of the pain that they give up. South Asian women also have a high risk of death from heart disease. Despite all that life throws at us as women, we still have to cope and

carry on. Things do get better, and we have to accept all of life's ups and downs, knowing that God still loves us.

This is a very important shabad to learn. When I moved to East London and lived alone for a year, I used to try and learn kirtan at Damesh Darbar Gurdwara by Seetal Singh Sitara. This is the first shabad he taught me at Damesh Darbar before I got married. This shabad is also one that Hardial Singh, who set up Guru Nanak Healing, recommends listening to every day:

'I am in peace when rising, in peace when sitting and feel no fear, when I realize that: The One Lord, who is the knower of all hearts, is my Protector. Care-free I sleep and unanxiously I awake realising that Thou, O Lord, art working everywhere in all. Says Nanak, the Guru has enshrined the Holy Word in my heart:
I live in peace within and without'
Guru Arjan Dev JI

When You Love Nature;
Nature Will Love You Back

Sometimes the demands of working and marriage are overwhelming. I reached a point where I wanted to escape the pressures of work and family.

I felt the need to connect to a greater force, and I left home for four weeks and went to New Mexico to mediate and exercise. I remember doing two hours of meditation early in the morning, and only then, did I feel that my heart was touched and opened. Sometimes, we go through life carrying so much pain, and in order to blunt the hurt, we close our hearts. When we do so, we think we have toughened, but we fail to realize the beauty in our lives. For example, beauty is viewing birds in motion, as well as the scenic and natural idyllic landscape.

The heart is where God resides, so look after your heart:

> **'The best place is your heart
> where God resides'**
> *Sukhmani Sahib Guru Arjan Dev Ji*

BREATHING

I often walk in nature, and it helps me clear my mind, thereby giving me a chance to think clearly. If you can listen to Nitnem and walk, this can help to clear all anxieties. You will enjoy clarity of thought and be at total peace with the self. This, of course, will also be reflected in your facial expression—the way you appear to others. We sometimes carry around many burdens, and they affect us in different ways, but through prayer, exercise, and contemplation, you can enjoy other benefits, such as the great aura you exude, which others will admire and even try to emulate. Listening and reading Gurbani helps clear all of our troublesaway so that we are free like a bird. If you can, gently breathe out—breathe out all of your worries as you walk. I have found that breathing out gently as you walk helps remove pain within the body. When I had my second son at home with no medical intervention or pain killers, my only support for controlling the pain was simply breathing out slowly.

FAITH

One strategy to help reduce stress is listening or reading the Jap Ji in the morning. Just as you clean your teeth every morning to get rid of the dirt, you need to clean your mind so that you can think properly. Also, it puts you in the right frame of mind to deal with life. Jap Ji is a journey toward the beauty of being with the Creator. Remember, you too are on a journey toward the Creator. Thus, all the struggles and joys will lead to peace within.

If you do not know how to read, listening to the words will help enormously.

If time does not permit other options, then listen to Jap JI on the way to work.

Listening has numerous benefits:
By Listening, pain and sin are erased.
By Listening, you dive deep into the ocean of virtue.
By Listening, the Shaykhs, religious scholars, spiritual teachers and emperors.
By Listening, even the blind find the Path.
By Listening, the Unreachable comes within your grasp.

'O Nanak, the devotees are forever in bliss'
Guru Nanak Dev Ji

After having an enlarged heart and other heart problems, my Uncle used to come to the Gurdwara to listen to Sukhmani Sahib. He found that after regular readings of Sukhmani Sahib, he experienced healing and peace. Hardial Singh's younger brother, Dr. Balwant Singh, is a medical doctor, and he found that again and again people were being healed by Gurbani and listening to Sukhmani Sahib. Dr. Balwant Singh diagnosed people before doing prayers and then afterward, and he found that many of them were cured of illnesses and diseases. Dr. Balwant then started running camps worldwide with much success. Many have been cured; however, those who were destined to leave this world left in peace and with poise.

There was a time when my own marriage was on the rocks, and I found it hard to cope and wanted to give up. However, after ringing a Sikhhelpline, they told me to sing in front of the sangat and everything would be all right. Thus, for the first time in my life, I plucked up the courage and sang the following shabad on the stage:

Kar Kirpa Prabh Deen Deelya

God is perfect - He is the Inner-knower, the Searcher of hearts.
He blesses us with the gift of the
dust of the feet of the Saints. ||1||
Bless me with Your Grace, God, O Merciful to the meek.
I seek Your Protection, O Perfect Lord,
Sustainer of the World. ||1||Pause||
He is totally pervading and permeating
the water, the land and the sky.
God is near at hand, not far away. ||2||
One whom He blesses with His Grace, meditates on Him.
Twenty-four hours a day, he sings the
Glorious Praises of the Lord. ||3||
He cherishes and sustains all beings and creatures.
Nanak seeks the Sanctuary of the Lord's Door.
||4||4||

By Guru Nanak Dev Ji

After singing this on the stage, I made a pact with the sangat that from then on I would seek the protection of the compassionate Creator. After this, I had no more problems. You will receive support. Sometimes the support you receive is not what you wanted, but HE is providing for you and deciding what you need at a particular time.

Always seek the light in the darkness, know that you have light of Waheguru within you
Gurmit Kaur

TATI VAO NA LAGEE
Tati Vao Na Lagee provides a circle of protection for you and your family. It was given to me by my mum when my baby son kept crying in the night. The shabad helped to settle and calm my younger son in the night. In addition to this, it helped me when my child was going through a difficult phase. Eventually, after a few months, he settled down.

This shabad is useful to learn by heart for protection for yourself:

*The hot wind doesn't blow over one
who has the Guru's protection.*

*The Lord's protecting circle is on all four sides
— pain and sorrow do not bother me, o brother.*

*I have met the perfect Satguru,
Who has made me as He wanted.*

*He gave me the medicine of God's Name,
and I am in tune with Him.*

The Protector has saved me, and cured all my sickness.

*Nanak says, "The Lord has given
His grace and support to me."*

By Guru Arjan Dev JI

Guru Amar Das Ji ' Gurmukhs continually peck at the Nam like swans pecking at pearls in the ocean'.

BRIDE OF THE UNIVERSE
In life as Sikhs, we should strive to be the brides of the Creator Waheguru, and this applies to both males and females. There will be times in your life when things do not always go as planned and you are alone. But it is those very times when you must build and nurture your relationship with Waheguru, because in the end, he is your Husband in this life and the next.

'Blessed is that happy soul-bride, O Nanak, who, as Gurmukh, seeks and finds the Lord'
Guru Amar Daas Ji

When you feel neglected and suffer in this world, this is the very time that you should seek the support of Waheguru:

*Where there is no mother, father,
children, friends or siblings
O my mind, there, only the Naam,
the Name of the Lord,
shall be with you as your help and support.
Where the great and terrible
Messenger of Death shall try to crush you,
there, only the Naam shall go along with you
Where the obstacles are so very heavy,
The Name of the Lord shall rescue you in an instant.*

Guru Arjan Dev Ji

CASE STUDY H: SARDANA AGED 39

This is a case study of a European lady who stumbled into Sikhi, fell in love, and never left it, and who married a Sikh man because he was Sikh. She wanted to be close to her new faith, and what better way to do this than to marry a Sikh man? Her man was rich but not rich enough to let her go to the Gurdwara alone. He was insecure and kept her in the house away from everyone. He tortured her and raped her. He was married before, but he never supported his first wife and children. She thought she was marrying into the Sikh faith as a European. She left disappointed and healed her wounds through a Sikh women's centre that supported her and gave her the courage to continue in her faith again and to live. She moved to the capital and lived alone until she met another Sikh man. Again, she fell in love with his love for Sikhi; she fell in love with his devotion, and it was something that they could share—the prayers and the meditation. She met him via a dating agency. His parents were devoted Sikhs and spent much of their time involved in the Gurdwara. He was divorced, but his ex-wife lived close by and his son visited often. However, he let her down by cancelling the engagement and then going missing a week before the wedding. She was left devastated, not knowing how he was or what had happened to him.

She was a European who had grown up in a Christian environment and suffered at the hands of a Sikh male, but she did not give up her Sikh faith. She separated her faith from the Sikh male. She knew her true husband was theLord Creator. That is our ultimate goal, despite all of thechallenges that we will face, including many that have not been coveredin this book. Remember that your true husband is the Creator, Lord Waheguru, and everyone else will leave you in the end. Your life on this earth is preparation to be wedded to the Creator and to enjoy limitless peace and joy.

Look at nature, even dead logs grow new life on them. Never give up on the Creator.
Gurmit Kaur

Gurmit Kaur

BE CREATIVE

THE WEDDING DAY

The day and hour of the marriage (departure to the next world) is fixed, so the friends should pour the customary oil on the threshold.

> ***Bless the bride, so that union with***
> ***the Master may be obtained.***
> ***Guru Nanak Dev Ji***

This is the big day, after which your life will change forever. Your life will no longer be yours; you will have to embrace your role as a woman in society. That role is very important; it is the foundation of communities.

I was extremely naïve when I first got married. I was no more than a simple girl, and everything changed overnight. I learned the hard way, and it was very tough. But throughout, I never gave up on my faith in God that one day everything would turn out all right. In the very long term it did. I met the man I should have married, and he respected me and taught me about life.

The wedding day is what most people prepare for with intricate detail, spending thousands on the display. However, the real challenge is accepting that this life you have is yours so that you can merge with the Creator, the Lord of the Universe:

> *'Nanak gives this advice:*
> *O beloved mind, without the Lord,*
> *all outward show is false'*
> *Guru Arjan Dev Ji*

Thus, your wedding day is essentially your preparation to be with God. You will no longer be one person, but two individuals with one soul, going on the journey to the Creator.

> *"They are not said to be husband and wife,*
> *who merely sit together. Rather they alone are*
> *called husband and wife, who have one soul*
> *in two bodies."*
> *(Guru Amar Das, Pauri, pg. 788)*

Once you prepare yourself and go to the Gurdwara, you will need to wait separately while the Milini and tea ceremony take place. Sometimes it is a very long wait, and it helps to wear a simple wedding dress to reduce the discomfort of waiting.

Once you enter the Darbar Sahib, you will be supported and directed by relatives to sit before the Siri Guru Granth Sahib. As you do so, first bow before the Siri Guru Granth Sahib.

One of the first shabads you will hear is 'KeetaLordie Kam So HarPeAkhiye'.The meaning of the shabad is provided below:

Keeta Lordie Kam So Har Pe Akhiye

"Whatever work you wish to accomplish-tell it to the Lord"

SHABAD OF GURU NANAK

*Which is the swan, and which is the crane?
It is only by His Glance of Grace.
Whoever is pleasing to Him, O Nanak,
is transformed from a crow into a swan.
Whatever work you wish to accomplish-tell it to the Lord.
He will resolve your affairs;
the True Guru gives His Guarantee of Truth.
In the Society of the Saints, you shall taste
the treasure of the Ambrosial Nectar.
The Lord is the Merciful Destroyer of fear;
He preserves and protects His slaves.
O Nanak, sing the Glorious Praises of the Lord,
and see the Unseen Lord God.
(Guru Granth Sahib Page 91)*

In Sikhi, we grasp the hem of the Lord in everything that we do. This is symbolised in the wedding: as we grasp the hem of our husband on this Earth, we remember that our true husband is the Creator, the Lord. Thus, as we reach out and let our father tie our hand to our husband's robe, we must remember on the spiritual level who our real Husband is—the one who gave us our life and looked after us all these years. As you grasp hold of HIS hem, you hold onto HIM as your support in life. As you hold onto HIM in support, you are affected by neither praise nor slander. These words will pass you. Let them not touch you, surround yourself with HIS love, and only praise the Creator. This may seem hard, but try to forget all of your past relationships with your family as you adjust to your new family. This seems really harsh because you have known and loved your family for your whole life. How on earth can you forget them? You have to focus on adjusting to your new family now.

Palle Tenda Lagee
"I have grasped hold of the hem of Your robe, Lord"
I have totally discarded praise and slander, O Nanak; I have forsaken and abandoned everything.
I have seen that all relationships are false, and so I have grasped hold of the hem of Your robe, Lord.
I wandered and wandered and went crazy, O Nanak, in countless foreign lands and pathways.
But then, I slept in peace and comfort, when I met the Guru, and found my Friend. ||2||
When I forget You, I endure all pains and afflictions.
Making thousands of efforts, they are still not eliminated.
One who forgets the Name, is known as a poor person.
One, who forgets the Name, wanders in reincarnation.
One who does not remember his Lord and Master, is punished by the Messenger of Death.
One who does not remember his Lord and Master, is judged to be a sick person.
One who does not remember his Lord and Master, is egotistical and proud.

One who forgets the Name is miserable in this world. ||14||

Shabad of Guru Arjan Dev JI

THE LAVAN

The Lavan ceremony is a spiritual ceremony that describes the stages of growth in spirituality.

The first Lavan asks you to learn righteousness through Gurus' words and to meditate on theName of the Lord.

In the second Lavan, as you meditate and adjust to your new life, your fear departs. You slowly begin to know your Creator, the soul of the Universe.

In the third Lavan, in the company of saints, you have finally awakened the love in your heart for the Lord and for your family. True love is not instant. Instant love comes and goes quickly; true love grows over time.

In the final stage, we are completely absorbed in the sweetness of our Beloved Creator within our mind, body, and soul. You have now truly become the bride of the Creator. That is your purpose in life, and through your marriage to the Creator, in your next life you will be at peace.

English Translation of the Marriage Hymns (Lavan)

By the first nuptial circling
The Lord showeth ye His Ordinance
for the daily duties of wedded life:
The Scriptures are the Word of the Lord,
Learn righteousness through them,
And the Lord will free ye from sin.
Hold fast to righteousness,
Contemplate the Name of the Lord,
Fixing it in your memory as the
Scriptures have prescribed.
Devote yourself to the Perfect and True Guru,
And all your sins shall depart.
Fortunate are those whose minds
Are imbued with the Sweetness of His Name,
To them happiness comes without effort;
The slave Nanak proclaimeth
That in the first circling(Round)
The marriage rite hath begun.

By the second nuptial circling (Round)
Ye are to understand that the Lord
Hath caused ye to meet the True Guru,
The fear in your heart has departed,
The filth of selfness in your minds is washed away,
By having the fear of God
and by singing His Praises.
I stand before Him with reverence,
The Lord God is the soul of the universe:
There is naught that He doth not pervade.
Within us and without, there is One God only:
In the company of Saints
Then are heard the songs of rejoicing.

The slave Nanak proclaimeth
That in the second circling
Divine Music is heard.
In the third circling
There is a longing for the Lord
And detachment from the world.
In the company of the Saints,
By our great good fortune,
We encounter the Lord.
The Lord is found in His purity
Through His exaltation,
Through the singing of His hymns.
By great good fortune we have lighted,
On the company of the Saints
Wherein is told the story
Of the Ineffable Lord.
The Holy Name echoes in the heart,
Echoes and absorbs us:
We repeat the Name of the Lord,
Being blessed by a fortunate destiny
Written from of old on our foreheads.
The slave Nanak proclaimeth
That in the third circling
The love of God has been awakened in the heart.
In the fourth circling
The mind reaches to knowledge of the Divine
And God is innerly grasped:
Through the Grace of the Guru
We have attained with ease to the Lord;
The sweetness of the Beloved
Pervades us, body and soul.
Dear and pleasing is the Lord to us:
Night and day our minds are fixed on Him.
By exalting the Lord

We have attained the Lord:
The fruit our hearts desired;
The Beloved has finished His work.
The soul, the spouse, delighteth in the Beloved's Name.
Felicitations fill our minds;
The Name rings in our hearts:b
The Lord God is united with His Holy Bride.
The heart of the Bride flowers with His Name.
The slave Nanak proclaimeth
That in the fourth circling
We have found the Eternal Lord.

These verses summarize the values and virtues of Anand Karaj. In fact, these verses are the stages of the journey toward unity with God.

The above interpretation has been taken from 'The Sikh Missionary Society'.

Shabad, "*Vivah hoa mere Babla*"
After the four stages, you are now one with the Creator. You are now married to the Lord of the Universe as a Gurmukh. You have found the jewels within your mind. The Creator exists within the mind, and through seva and simran, you are now enlightened.

This is the time to celebrate because there is no duality of existence.

VIVAH HOA MERE BABLA...."
My marriage has been performed.
As a Gurmukh I have found the Lord
The darkness of ignorance has been dispelled.
The Guru has revealed the blazing light of spiritual wisdom
My marriage has been performed
I have found the priceless Jewel of Lord
The sickness of my ego has been dispelled
Through the Gurus Teachings my identity has been joined with my true identity
I have obtained my Husband Lord
He is imperishable

There are many shabads that are sung after the Sikh marriage ceremony. The most common one is *'Poori Asa Ji Mansa Mere Ram'*. This is beautiful only because it sings of the joy and happiness of having found your true husband within your own home.

That is, within yourself as the Creator, you are the light of the Creator, now that you have discovered the Creator within yourself.

<u>*POORI ASA JI MANSA MERE RAM*</u>
"My hopes and desires have been fulfilled, O my Lord"

Shabad of Guru Arjan

My hopes and desires have been fulfilled, O my Lord.
I am worthless, without virtue; all virtues are Yours, O Lord.
All virtues are Yours, O my Lord and Master; with what mouth should I praise You?

You did not consider my merits and demerits; you forgave me in an instant.
I have obtained the nine treasures, congratulations are pouring in, and the unstruck melody resounds.
Says Nanak, I have found my Husband Lord within my own home, and all my anxiety is forgotten.
(Guru Granth Sahib Page 576)

Picture of the bride merging with the Universe. Each clog on the painting represents the Lavan stages that we have to go through as a Sikh before we become brides of the Universe.

RESOURCES AND SUPPORT

Sikh Faith Based support group for women.

Website:
http://www.sikhsanjog.com/

Contact:
info@sikhsanjog.com

SIKH HELPLINE
We are here to talk:

If you have any questions or enquiries, we are here to talk. No question is too silly, and you can use the form below to contact us here at Sikh Helpline, and we will reply as soon as possible.

Alternatively you can use your own email and contact us at; info@sikhhelpline.com.

CALL: 0845 644 0704 (UK)
MOBILE: 07999 004 363 (UK)
EMAIL: info@sikhhelpline.com
86 Birmingham St, Oldbury, West Midlands,
B69 4EB
Sikh Awareness Society
http://www.sasorg.co.uk/

Contact Us
General Enquiries: 07780 601 351

Further information, Sewa opportunities, Event bookings etc: sas.helpline@googlemail.com

Serious Enquiries Only:
07780 601 351
07961 522 713
07871 543 495
07782 209 193

If you are a victim of hate-crime, or are facing problems highlighted by the SAS and require assistance. sas.helpline@googlemail.com

The Sikh Community Care Project (SCCP) was set up in 1997 by a team of local volunteers in the Waltham Forest area. Services include advice, support and a variety of health, social, recreation & cultural activities for people from all over the community.

Venue address:
Argyle Road, Ilford, Essex IG1 3BG

Telephone:
020 8554 3377

Email:
sccpredbridge@yahoo.co.uk

Website:
http://sikhcommunitycp.bttradespace.com

MASSIS BLESSING TO YOU

May you always be blessed and surrounded by love
May God give you continual strength
so that you can give strength
Remember there is good in everyone, learn to find it
Whatever happens always keep your heart open

FORGIVENESS FOR MISTAKES
Please forgive me for any mistakes I have made. I wrote this guide to help young women ease their way into married life and to support them with Sikhi as a guide. The guidance is based on our Guru's teachings, and our Guru is immortal and an embodiment of God on Earth. I am only a mortal servant and unworthy, however; our Guru's teachings are worthy and worth abiding by, so please reflect upon them to obtain and create love within your households.

www.ingramcontent.com/pod-product-compliance
Lightning Source LLC
Chambersburg PA
CBHW020948090426
42736CB00010B/1318